Control Systems

How the Nervous System Works

DEVELOPED IN COOPERATION
WITH
OMAHA CHILDREN'S MUSEUM
OMAHA, NEBRASKA

Copyright © 1995 by Scholastic Inc.   All rights reserved. Published by Scholastic Inc.   Printed in the U.S.A.
ISBN 0-590-27666-2
2 3 4 5 6 7 8 9 10   09   01 00 99 98 97 96 95

THE HUMAN BODY IS MADE UP OF COMPLEX SYSTEMS THAT INTERACT TO KEEP AN INDIVIDUAL ALIVE.

Control Systems

The nervous system controls many of the functions of the body.

The nervous system gathers information about the environment through the sense organs.

The brain, spinal cord, and nerves transmit signals that control the body.

A person makes decisions that affect the health of the nervous system.

Think Tank: Designing a Robot Exploration Lab

Your Own Personal Computer

Your brain is truly amazing. The biggest computers can't do all the things your brain can do—and your brain is small. It weighs only about 1.5 kilograms (about 3 pounds), just a tiny fraction of what the most powerful computers weigh.

Your brain and your nerves are parts of the body systems that control everything you do. These control systems allow you to taste foods and to hear music. They make it possible for you to read the words on this page, to blink, to breathe.

What do you know about your control systems?

Even if you don't know exactly how your brain and senses work, you probably know some things about them. Work with your class to make a list of what you already know.

What do you want to know?

Make a second list with your class. This time, list questions you have about your brain and senses. You could start your list with a question about the picture on the next page: Why doesn't everybody see the same thing when they look at this picture?

How will you find out?

You'll work in teams to discover many of the answers to your questions. You'll share what you learn with other teams in your class. You'll also find out what other scientists have discovered about the control systems.

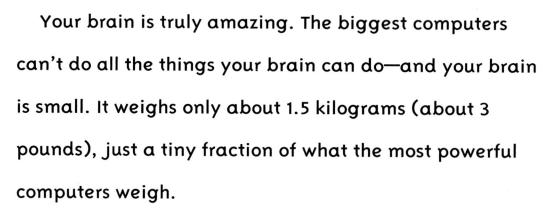

Using scientific methods:

Take a close look at the table of contents. Each lesson title is a problem you're going to solve. Each problem you solve will help you solve the ones that come after it. In each lesson, you and your class will use scientific methods to solve the problem:

- You'll make a *hypothesis* – a prediction – about possible answers to the problem.

- You'll do a *hands-on exploration* – sometimes two of them – that will help test your hypothesis.

- You'll *record data* you collect.

- You'll *draw conclusions* from your data.

- You'll *compare* your conclusions with those of other teams in your class.

- You'll *apply* your conclusions to your own life.

The Video Mystery will help you get started.

How Do You Get Information?

You don't just live in the world, you react to it all the time. You react to what's going on around you, even while you're sleeping. Right now—without you thinking about it—your brain is getting information about lots of things that are happening. How do you think your brain gets information about your surroundings?

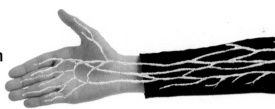

Exploration:
Discover what's in the box.

You need:

Mystery box

❶ Think of the ways you identify objects. How can you use those ways to help you identify the contents of the box?

❷ Use any methods that will help you find out what's in the box. There's only one rule: You must not open the box. Record any observations you make. ✐

❸ Use what you've learned to guess what's in the box.

Interpret your results.

- What parts of your body did you use in your investigation?

- What special jobs do those parts of your body do?

- How could you tell how many items were in the box?

- What did you do to identify the items? Compare methods with your classmates.

- Ask your teacher what's in the box. Was your guess about the contents correct? What clues did you use to guess the identity of each item?

- If your guess was not correct, why wasn't it? Why couldn't you figure out what was in the box?

▲ The human nervous system

How did you try to find out what was in the mystery box? How do you know what's going on around you at this very minute? The answer to both questions is the same. You use your <u>sense organs</u>—your eyes, ears, nose, tongue, and skin—to be aware of your surroundings. Your sense organs help you to see, hear, smell, taste, and feel.

The sense organs can't do their jobs all alone. They're part of the <u>nervous system</u> and work with the other parts of this system. Find the <u>brain</u> in the diagram. The brain is the control center. It's connected by <u>nerves</u> to all parts of your body. A few nerves connect directly to the brain. Find these nerves. Where in the body are they? The rest of the nerves are linked to the brain by the thick <u>spinal cord</u>. Can you find it?

Here's how the nervous system works to let you hear. When there's a sound near you, your ears send off signals. The signals travel along nerves to your brain. When the signals reach a place called the hearing center of the brain, you hear. If something stopped the signals from getting there, you wouldn't hear even though your ears were working perfectly. The brain has a different center for receiving signals from each kind of sense organ.

The brain sends signals, too. Most of these signals travel over nerves to muscles and cause them to move. Signals that travel inside the brain let you think, remember, and imagine.

If you had a stone in your shoe, signals would travel from the skin touching the stone to the brain. Look at the diagram and tell how the signals might get there. How would you get signals that would cause you to get rid of the stone? Find a path on the diagram that these signals might follow.

Your nervous system is like many busy highways. The signals that travel to and from your brain are the traffic. It's amazing there are no traffic jams. Just think how many things you notice and how many muscles you move every moment. You use 17 muscles just to smile. Your senses are always at work, keeping you aware of what's happening. You often have to use more than one sense at the same time. Do you think you could tell the difference between a lemon and a lime using only your sense of touch?

Exploration:
Use your senses.

You need:
Cotton balls
Socks
Mystery bag 1
Mystery bag 2

❶ Use cotton balls to make an earplug for each ear. Put in both earplugs, put the socks on your hands, and close your eyes.

❷ Ask your partner to give you the items from bag 1. Hold one in each hand. Make observations about each item from the way it feels. Have your partner record your observations.

❸ Smell each of the mystery items carefully. Have your partner record any observations you can make.

❹ Take off the socks and feel the items. Then take out your earplugs. Have your partner record any new observations you make.

❺ Open your eyes and observe the items.

❻ Trade places and have your partner do steps 1–5 with the items in bag 2.

Interpret your results.

• Did you identify either of the items before step 5? How?

• Did you need to use a combination of senses to identify an item? Why?

Closer to Home: Our best friend

Like you, many animals rely on their senses to get information. And like you, they can share the information with others. If our senses aren't as sharp as we want them to be, we can sometimes have animals help us.

Dogs make great pets, but some of them have jobs too. You probably know about police dogs and dog guides that help people who have trouble seeing or can't see at all. Did you know there are also service dogs that help people who don't hear well? If you see a dog with a yellow or orange collar and leash, it's probably a hearing dog. The dog is taught to warn its owner of dangers that can be heard, such as smoke alarms. It also lets its owner know when it hears such things as the telephone or the doorbell. The dog begins the five- or six-month training when it's about one year old. And after the dog's training, its owner is also taught how to look after this new friend and helper.

- When might dog owners who aren't deaf rely on their animals' sense of hearing?

- How do you think your sense of smell compares to a dog's sense of smell? How do you know?

- How else do people use dogs to help them? Which of the dogs' senses help them in each job?

▲ This hearing dog is helping its owner by waking her up when the alarm rings.

▼ Bloodhounds can sometimes pick up a person's trail four days after it was made.

What signals from your sense organs might your brain respond to while you're asleep?

How Do Signals Travel Through Your Nervous System?

Signals are traveling in your nervous system all the time. Your sense organs are sending signals and your brain is, too. Like all the other parts of your body, your nervous system is made up of the small living units called cells. <u>Nerve cells</u> do the work of the nervous system. They send signals from sense organs. The signals travel through nerve cells along nerves. And nerve cells in the brain receive and send signals. How do you think signals travel along nerves?

Exploration:
Make a model showing how a signal travels.

You need:
Plastic fork
Pencil
Marble
Dominoes

❶ Arrange the fork, pencil, and marble as shown in the photograph. The fork handle should be up in the air, and the marble should just touch the tines of the fork.

❷ Set up a line of 12 dominoes standing on end, 4 cm apart from each other. The last domino should be 4 cm away from the raised end of the fork.

❸ Tap the first domino and observe what happens.

Interpret your results.

• The model you made stands for a nerve, the brain, and the brain's response. In your experiment, a signal is sent from a sense organ to the brain. Which part of the model stands for the brain?

• What does the line of dominoes stand for?

• What could the marble stand for?

• When you knocked over one domino, what happened to the next domino? How might this show how a signal travels along a nerve?

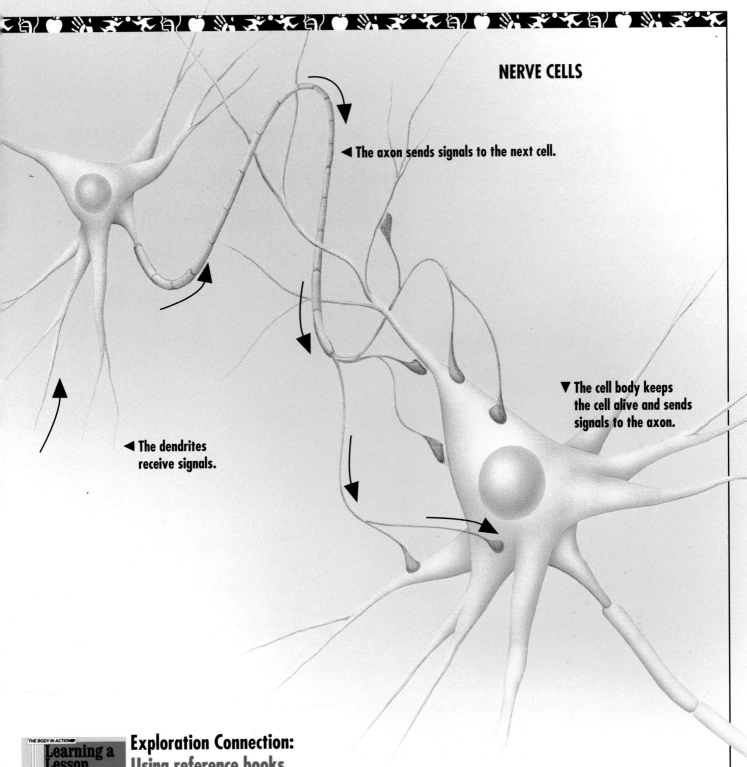

◄ The axon sends signals to the next cell.

◄ The dendrites receive signals.

▼ The cell body keeps the cell alive and sends signals to the axon.

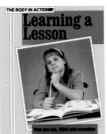

Exploration Connection:
Using reference books

There are billions of nerve cells in your nervous system. A nerve is a bundle of nerve cells held together by a covering, like the wires in a cable. Each of the long, wirelike parts of a nerve is made of nerve cells arranged in a row, one after the other. When a signal travels along a nerve, it moves from one nerve cell to the next in one of these rows of cells. How does this remind you of the way the dominoes in your model nerve moved?

Study the brain nerve cells above to learn how a signal travels. Which part of a nerve cell receives a signal? Which part passes the signal to the next cell? There's a very small space between the end of one cell and the beginning of the next. How does a signal get across this space? You can find out by reading pages 14–15 of *Learning a Lesson*.

You see a tennis ball coming toward you. You raise your racket and smash the ball. What's needed to carry out this action? Signals must travel from your eye to the vision center of your brain. Your brain must decide what your body should do and send signals to the muscles of your arm. Of course, all the signals travel from nerve cell to nerve cell. How long do you think the whole thing takes? The least amount of time it takes to respond to something you see is your reaction time. How fast is your reaction time?

Exploration:
Test how fast you react.

You need:
Sheet of paper

❶ Have your partner hold a sheet of paper at the top between thumb and forefinger, as shown in the photograph.

❷ Hold your own thumb and forefinger between 7 and 8 cm below the top of the paper, but don't touch the paper.

❸ Without warning you, your partner will let go of the paper. Try to catch it between your thumb and forefinger. Do not move your hand up or down.

❹ Try this test several times. Then trade places and test your partner's reaction time.

Interpret your results.

• Did you close your fingers as soon as you saw the paper falling?

• Did you catch the paper?

• It takes the average person about one fifth of a second to react and close the thumb and forefinger. Do you think you reacted in less time, or more?

• How could you find out if your reaction time gets better with practice? **Try it!**

▲ Most sports require fast reactions.

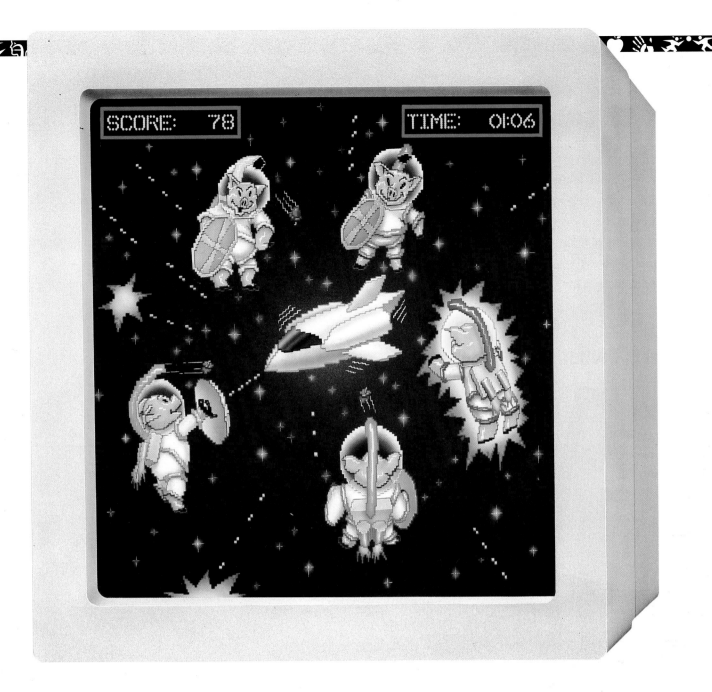

Closer to Home:
Video games

Have you ever played a video game? People who get great scores in a game have usually played it before. But it's likely that they react really fast, too.

In the video game shown on this page, you shoot cosmic acorns to each space pig before it decides to snack on your rocket ship. The space pigs keep showing up—faster and faster! In the first round of the game, there's one new pig each second. In the second round, there are two pigs each second. In the third round, there are three pigs each second, and so on. If you have a reaction time of one fifth of a second, how many rounds could you complete (if you made no mistakes)?

• What sense organs send signals to your brain when you play video games?

• What parts of your body must react quickly when you play video games?

• What are some other things you do that require you to react quickly?

Could the same nerve cell carry signals to and from your brain? Explain.

How Do You See?

If you want to hit a ball, you first have to be able to see it. You know which sense organs help you to see—your eyes do. But sometimes you can't see even though your eyes are wide open. That's because your eyes aren't sending signals to your brain. Why aren't they? What has to be in your surroundings for your eyes to work?

Exploration:
Find out what's needed for you to be able to see.

You need:
Colored markers
Index cards
Tape
Viewing box
Notebook paper

❶ Write a short secret message on an index card. Use several colors in your message. Don't let your partner see what you're writing.

❷ Tape your secret message inside the box, on the end that doesn't have the eyehole.

❸ Have your partner peek through the eyehole for 30 seconds. Then your partner should record as much of the secret message as he or she can, using colors to match the colors on the message. ✏

❹ Fold back the top sheet of notebook paper on top of the box and have your partner repeat step 3. ✏

❺ Fold back one sheet of paper each time your partner begins step 3, until there are no sheets of paper covering the hole on top of the box.

❻ Fold all the sheets of paper back over the hole and trade places. Go through steps 1–5 to read your partner's secret message.

Interpret your results.

• How did the number of sheets of paper over the hole affect what you could see in the box? What changed?

• If you can see an object, does that mean you can tell what color it is? Explain.

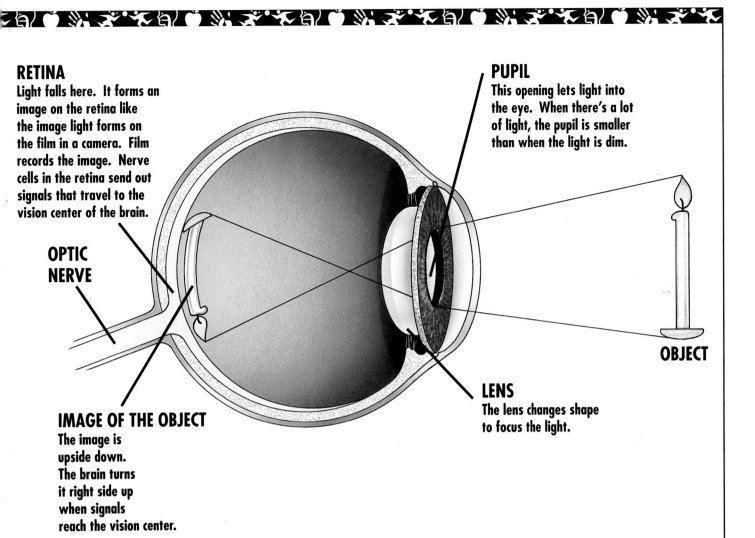

RETINA
Light falls here. It forms an image on the retina like the image light forms on the film in a camera. Film records the image. Nerve cells in the retina send out signals that travel to the vision center of the brain.

OPTIC NERVE

IMAGE OF THE OBJECT
The image is upside down. The brain turns it right side up when signals reach the vision center.

PUPIL
This opening lets light into the eye. When there's a lot of light, the pupil is smaller than when the light is dim.

OBJECT

LENS
The lens changes shape to focus the light.

Exploration Connection:
Using reference books

When light falls on an object, some of the light bounces off it. This reflected light is what makes it possible for you to see what's around you. When light reflected off an object enters your eye, the <u>lens</u> bends the light rays and focuses them on the <u>retina</u>. The retina is a layer of nerve cells that lines the inside of the eye at the back of the eyeball.

Trace the path of each light ray shown as a line in the diagram. Start where the light leaves the candle. How do the light rays get into the eye? What happens to each ray as it passes through the lens? Why is the image formed by the light rays on the retina upside down?

The nerve cells of the retina react to the light falling on them by sending signals. They travel over the optic nerves to the vision center of the brain. Then you see the object.

Each retina has two kinds of nerve cells that respond to light. They are named for their shapes—rod cells and cone cells. Rod cells work in dim light. They let you see shades of gray. Cone cells need bright light and let you see colors. To find out more about these cells, turn to pages 48–50 of *Looking at Senses*.

Each of your eyes works the same way. If that's true, what's the advantage of having two eyes?

Exploration:
Observe how your eyes work together.

You need:
Index card
Penny
Paper cup

❶ Work with a partner. Cover your right eye with the index card.

❷ Direct your partner to move the hand holding the penny until you think it is above the cup. Use the directions "left," "right," "toward me," or "away from me." Then have your partner drop the penny.

❸ Repeat the activity. This time, cover your left eye and use your right eye.

❹ Repeat the activity with both your eyes uncovered.

Interpret your results.

• What differences did you notice in steps 2, 3, and 4?

• How would you describe what is special about your vision when you use both eyes?

• How do you think having two eyes helps you thread a needle? How does it help you in sports?

▼ Even when you're looking straight ahead, you can also see off to the sides.

Closer to Home:
Seeing is believing.

Your eyes allow you to look at objects near and far, and to notice the difference between them. When you look in front of you, which part of the view is clearest? How wide is the view? Here's one way to find out. Look straight ahead with one index finger on each side of your head. Wiggle your fingers as you slowly move them back toward your ears. How far back are your fingers when you can't see them? **Try it!**

Each of your eyes has a spot in the retina where there are no nerve cells. This spot is at the point where the nerve that sends signals to your brain connects to the retina. You can make the cat or the mouse disappear

when you find this "blind spot." Close your left eye and hold this book close to your face. Stare directly at the mouse. Can you see the cat, too? Slowly move the book away from your face while staring at the mouse. The cat should disappear for a second. **Try it!** If you close your right eye and stare at the cat, you can make the mouse disappear.

- Your vision is sharpest when light focuses on the part of the retina that has the most nerve cells. Where do you think this part of the retina is?

- Why don't you notice your blind spot when both of your eyes are open?

Think!

Some kinds of animals that spend their entire lives in dark caves have no eyes at all! Would they be able to see if they did have eyes? Explain.

17

How Do You Hear?

Even though your vision covers quite a lot of space, you can't see behind you. But you know when the person at the desk behind you drops a book. You use more than just your sense of sight to be aware of what's going on all around you. Your sense of hearing tells you that the book dropped. Have you ever seen a dog tip its head when it hears something? Why do you think the dog tips its head?

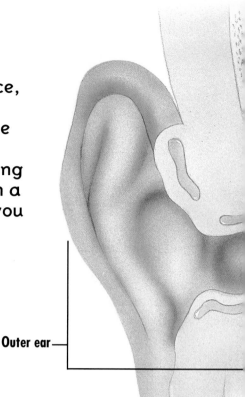

Outer ear

Exploration:
Put your ears to the test.

You need:
Cotton balls

❶ Use cotton balls to make an earplug for each ear. Put in both earplugs, and close your eyes.

❷ Have your partner snap his or her fingers about 1 m away from you. If you can hear the sound, try to figure out the direction it's coming from. Have your partner snap fingers at different points around you.

❸ Take the earplug out of one ear and repeat step 2. What can you do to help you determine the location of the sound?

❹ Take out both earplugs and repeat step 2.

Interpret your results.

• What do earplugs do?

• How well could you tell the direction of a sound when you had earplugs in both ears? in one ear only?

• What could you do to help you find the direction of a sound?

• Why do dogs tip their heads when they're listening to something?

• Each ear works the same way. How does having two ears help your sense of hearing?

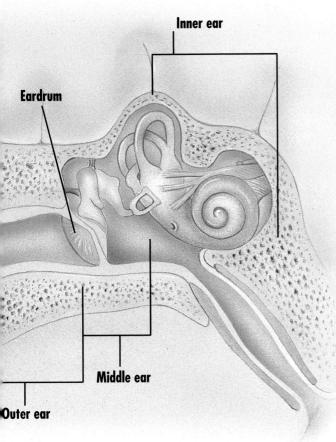

Inner ear

Eardrum

Middle ear

Outer ear

▲ With your finger, trace the path of sound from the outer ear to the inner ear.

Exploration Connection: Using reference books

Sounds are vibrations traveling through air. When you hear something, you're actually hearing air vibrate. Find the outer ear on the diagram. How do you think the shape of your outer ear helps your <u>eardrum</u> receive the air vibrations?

Sound travels from your eardrum to your inner ear. Find it on the diagram. How do you think a sound reaches the inner ear? Find the part of the inner ear that is coiled like a snail's shell. Inside this part are little hairs that are connected to nerve cells. When a sound moves the hairs, the nerve cells send out signals. They travel over your hearing nerve to the hearing center of your brain. You can find out more about your sense of hearing on pages 59–61 of *Looking at Senses*.

▶ A deer's safety may depend on its hearing.

Do you know that you should never put anything smaller than your curled-up fist into your ears? That's because it's very easy to damage your eardrums. So it's wise not to put things in your ears. Stiff things—such as pencils—are especially dangerous. Like a drum, an eardrum is a very thin, tightly-stretched tissue. How do your eardrums help you to hear?

Exploration:
Make a drum.

You need:
Plastic bowl
Plastic wrap
Tape
Sand
Baking tray

❶ Stretch a piece of plastic wrap tightly over the top of the bowl so there are no wrinkles. Tape the plastic wrap around the rim of the bowl.

❷ Spread a pinch of sand over the stretched plastic wrap.

❸ Bang a baking tray loudly just above the plastic wrap. Record your observations.

Interpret your results.

• What happened to the sand when you banged the tray?

• How do you think the plastic wrap was affected?

• Your eardrum is a thin piece of skin, and it's stretched very tightly. What do you think your eardrum does when sound reaches it?

Closer to Home:
Your hearing range

The vibrations that reach your eardrums aren't all the same. Think about striking piano keys. As you hit the keys farther and farther to the left, the sound gets lower and lower. As you move to the right, the sound gets higher and higher. If the piano had more keys that made higher and higher sounds, you'd finally reach sounds too high for you to hear. Your cat would hear them, though. In fact, many animals can hear sounds that are higher than the highest sounds humans can hear.

If the piano had more keys that made lower and lower sounds, you'd reach sounds that are too low for you to hear. Elephants might hear them—they can make and hear very low sounds. These low sounds travel farther than higher sounds. Elephants can hear each other at a distance of at least 4 kilometers (2 1/2 miles). Luckily, you can't hear these low sounds! If you could, you might also hear other low sounds, such as the noise your blood makes traveling through your body.

- There are machines that make noises that keep mice out of houses. Why do you think these machines don't bother the people who live in the houses?

- Can each of the animals on the chart hear anything you might hear? Why?

HEARING Range

Human Being	20 to 20,000 hertz
Bat	1,000 to 100,000 hertz
Cat	60 to 65,000 hertz
Dog	15 to 40,000 hertz
Robin	250 to 21,000 hertz
Dolphin	7 to 170,000 hertz

Think!

If you damaged an eardrum, how do you think it would change your hearing?

How Do You Detect Smells?

You hear a crash behind you. It sounds like a bottle breaking on the floor. But before you turn around to see what has happened, one of your other senses lets you know. A bottle of perfume has smashed open. How can your nose tell it's perfume and not paint?

Exploration:
Test your sense of smell.

You need:
Mystery cups 1–4
Lab Mat 6
Goggles

❶ Carefully smell the contents of cup 1. Record your observations about the smell on the LabMat by making a check next to each word that describes the smell. Add any other words that describe the smell.

❷ If the contents of the cup have only a faint scent, record what you do to help you smell them.

❸ Repeat step 1 for each of the other three cups.

Interpret your results.

• Could you tell if any of the contents would be good to eat? How?

• Were you able to identify any of the contents? How?

• Think about what you do when you try to smell something. How do you move your head? What do you do with your nose? How do you breathe in? Why?

• If you hold your nose and take in air through your mouth, can you still smell things? **Try it!**

▲ This garden is for the enjoyment of people who can't see well. The plants may not have bright flowers, but they have strong smells and surfaces that are interesting to touch. Signs in braille tell about the plants.

Exploration Connection: Using reference books

Smells are carried in the air you breathe. When you breathe in, odors are carried far up your nose. The endings of thousands of smelling nerves are grouped there. They react by sending signals to the smell center of your brain. Then you smell an odor.

Most smells are really mixes of many different smells. Bacon and vanilla, for example, are mixes of more than a hundred different smells. Perfumes and fragrances, too, are made by mixing different smells. Your brain can tell the difference between about 10,000 different odors. To find out more about how your sense of smell works, read pages 17–19 of *Looking at Senses*.

Think about the things you smelled in the activity. Suppose a friend mixed together two or three of those things in one container. If your eyes were closed, could you figure out what was mixed together in the container? **Try it!**

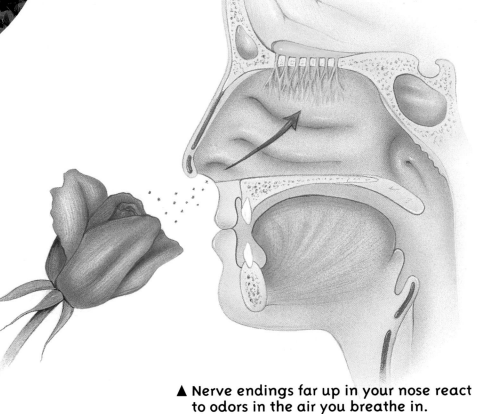

▲ Nerve endings far up in your nose react to odors in the air you breathe in.

Closer to Home:
Something smells fishy.

Your nose could save your life! Some things that you can't see or hear are dangerous. Gasoline fumes, for example, are poisonous to breathe, and they're explosive. It's a good thing you can smell them. Natural gas is used for cooking or heating homes. It's poisonous and explosive too, but it has no odor. The companies that provide natural gas to homes add a chemical that has a strong smell to the natural gas. This smell alerts you if there's a gas leak in your house.

The way a thing smells can tell you whether it's dangerous to you. Rotten food smells bad, and you avoid it. Many dangerous chemicals and fumes also smell bad to you, even if you don't know they're dangerous.

Car exhaust smells bad to nearly everyone. That's a good thing, too, because these fumes contain carbon monoxide. Carbon monoxide is a dangerous gas—it can kill. But it has no odor, so you may not know it's around you.

Factories may put dangerous chemicals into the air, but you can't tell if they're harmful just by looking.

How can you protect yourself against a gas you can't smell? One important way is to follow this rule: Never stay in a place where the gas could collect. Keep out of a garage when a car inside has its engine running. Outside, if you have to be in a stopped car with its engine running, open one or more of the car's windows. That way the gas can't collect inside the car.

- If you thought you smelled a faint odor of smoke in your house, what would you do to investigate its cause? How could you use your sense of smell to help?

- If there was a smell of natural gas in the house, what would you do to safeguard yourself?

- Suppose you were stuck in a bad traffic jam on a cold, windy day. What are two things you and the driver could do to protect yourselves from carbon monoxide poisoning?

Think!

If someone opens a bottle of perfume on the other side of the room, you can smell the perfume. Why?

◄ The smell of decaying meat warns you that eating it would be dangerous, but it wouldn't be dangerous to a vulture.

How Do You Detect Tastes?

Your sense of smell can help you know what's good to eat and what's not. Your sense of taste can do the same thing. How many tastes do you think there are? You might be surprised to find out that there are just four kinds of taste—salty, sour, sweet, and bitter. But many foods have a combination of two or more tastes. Where do you think your sense organs for taste are?

Exploration:
Map your tongue.

You need:

Mirror
4 solutions
Cotton swabs
Colored markers
Cup of water
Goggles

❶ Stick out your tongue and look at it in the mirror. Draw an outline of your tongue on a sheet of paper.

❷ Swirl a *clean* cotton swab around in the salty solution. Dab different areas of your tongue with the swab—the tip of the tongue, the edges, the middle, and the back. Use one colored marker to make spots on the outline of the tongue to show the areas of the tongue that responded strongly to the taste of the salt. *Throw away the swab.*

❸ Repeat step 2 for each liquid. *Use a fresh swab* for each taste, and rinse your mouth with water after each taste. Throw away the swabs after each use. Add to your taste map of the tongue, using a different color for each taste.

Interpret your results.

• Which parts of your tongue respond strongly to things that are salty? sweet? sour? bitter?

• Compare your tongue map with your friends' maps. How are they similar or different?

Exploration Connection:
Interpreting tables

Your mouth waters a little bit every time you eat something. The watery fluid in your mouth is saliva. As it spreads over your tongue, it covers the <u>taste</u> <u>buds</u>—the sense organs for taste. Nerves that begin in the taste buds send out signals when tiny bits of food dissolved in the saliva touch their endings. They send signals to the taste center of your brain. Then you get a taste.

The taste buds in different parts of your mouth react especially strongly to just one of the four tastes—sweet or salty or bitter or sour. If nerve endings in taste buds at the tip of your tongue send signals to your brain about food you're eating, how will the food taste to you?

The table shows how tastes are combined in some foods. What other foods could you add to the list? What combination of tastes do you think each of those foods has?

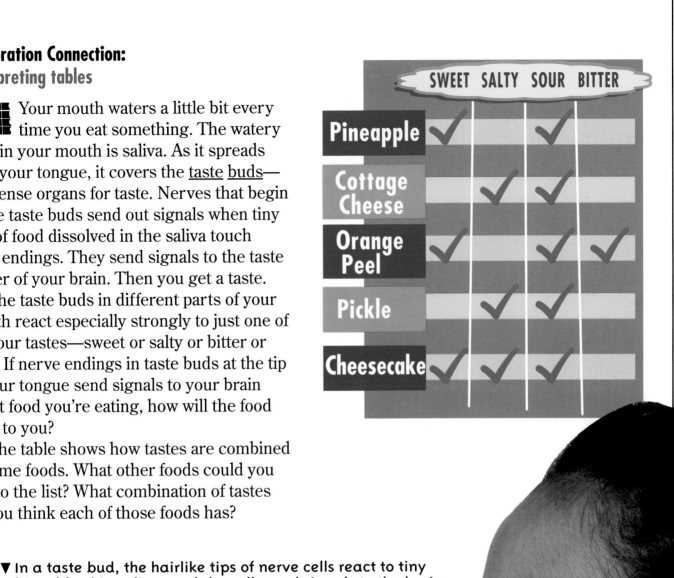

	SWEET	SALTY	SOUR	BITTER
Pineapple	✓		✓	
Cottage Cheese		✓	✓	
Orange Peel	✓		✓	✓
Pickle		✓	✓	
Cheesecake	✓	✓	✓	

▼ In a taste bud, the hairlike tips of nerve cells react to tiny bits of food in saliva, and the cells send signals to the brain.

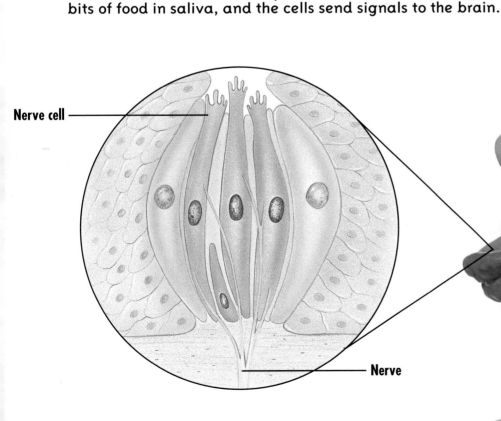

Nerve cell

Nerve

▶Blue cheese

▼ Hot peppers

▲ Olives

▲ Many people have to learn
to like the flavors of these
foods.

Closer to Home:
Flavor

What do you like most about your favorite food?
You'd probably answer its taste, but taste might be only
part of what you really like about the food. Think back to
the last time you had a cold and a stuffed-up nose. Most
likely, food didn't seem as good as usual. That's because
when you eat, you enjoy a mix of the food's taste and
smell. If you can't smell food as you eat it, you might not
even be able to tell what you're eating. And if food is
very cold or very hot, you won't get the full taste. That's
because your taste buds work better when your food is
at about the same temperature as your body.

Have you ever eaten any of the foods shown on these
pages? If you have, you may not have liked them when
you first tried them. Foods like olives, hot peppers,
anchovies, blue cheese, and brussels sprouts have flavors
that take some getting used to. But when people try them
a few times, they find that they enjoy these special flavors.

What you like to eat can depend on where you live. If you live in one of the southwestern states, you might like hot peppers better than anchovies. If you lived in Italy, you'd probably like olives a lot. Are there any special foods that your part of the country is known for? Do you think people from other states would enjoy them too?

- If you closed your eyes, could you tell the difference between a bite of apple and a bite of raw potato? **Try it!**

- Do you think you could tell the difference between a bite of apple and a bite of raw potato if you closed your eyes and held your nose? **Try it!**

- Which do you think tastes sweeter—frozen yogurt when it's still frozen or after it has melted?

◀ Anchovies

◀ Brussels sprouts

Think!

Many dogs love cookies, but most cats aren't interested in them. Why do you think that is?

How Does Your Sense of Touch Work?

When you dabbed your tongue with a cotton swab, you probably felt the swab touch your tongue. You might have felt its touch even in places where you couldn't taste anything. That means your tongue has more than one kind of sense detector. The touch detectors are part of the skin covering your tongue. Are there touch detectors in the skin covering other parts of your body?

Exploration:
Map your sense of touch.

You need:

Bent paper clip
Ruler

❶ Bend the paper clip to form a U, with the gap between the ends measuring 3 mm.

❷ Have your partner look away. Gently touch your partner's wrist with the two ends of the paper clip. Ask your partner if he or she felt a single touch or two touches, and record the answer. Try different spots on your partner's wrist.

❸ Test your partner's palm and fingertips. Be sure to use only a light touch each time. Test each area many times. Each time, record whether your partner can feel both ends of the paper clip or only one end.

❹ Trade places with your partner. Repeat steps 2 and 3.

Interpret your results.

• In which areas of your skin could you feel both ends of the paper clip?

• There are nerve endings in your skin that respond to touch. Which areas of your skin have the most nerve endings? How is this helpful?

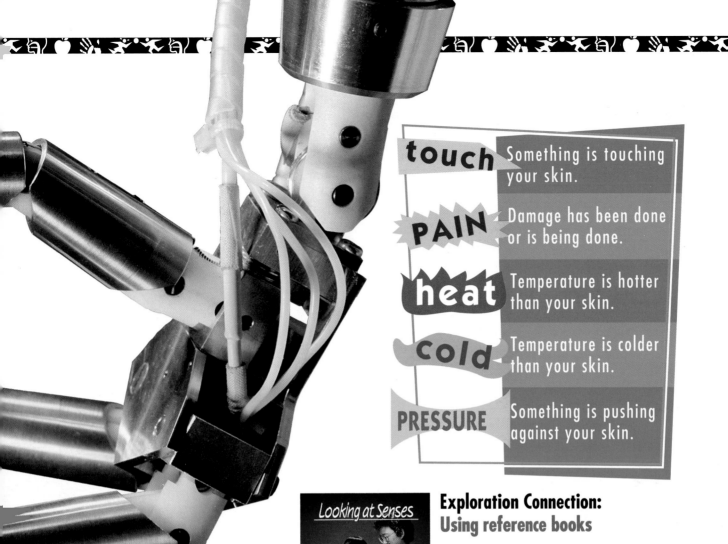

touch	Something is touching your skin.
PAIN	Damage has been done or is being done.
heat	Temperature is hotter than your skin.
cold	Temperature is colder than your skin.
PRESSURE	Something is pushing against your skin.

▲ It took a lot of time and money to make a robot that can hold an egg—but it still can't do it nearly as well as you can.

Looking at Senses

DAVID SUZUKI

Exploration Connection: Using reference books

In the Exploration, you tested your skin only for the kind of nerve ending that responds to touch. Your skin also has other kinds of nerve endings that send signals to your brain. When the signals reach the proper center of the brain, you feel pain or pressure or some other sensation. What you feel depends on which kind of nerve ending sent the signal. The table lists the different nerve endings that send signals about feeling.

Which kind of nerve ending would you depend on to let you know what's happening in each of the following situations? Would you depend on more than one kind of nerve ending for each situation?

- You turn on a faucet to wash your hands.

- You scrape your knee.

- A spider crawls up your arm.

- You shake hands with someone.

- You pick up an ice cube.

You can find out more about the nerve endings in your skin by reading pages 7–9 of *Looking at Senses*.

You discovered some parts of your body have a lot of nerve endings that respond to touch. Do you think that those parts have most of the other kinds of nerve endings too? If you want to test the temperature of bath water, do you use the parts of your body that have the most touch nerve endings? Or would you use another part of your body?

Exploration:
Map your heat and cold nerve endings.

You need:

2 metal spoons
Hot water
Ice water
Notebook paper
Washable ink pen
Paper towel

❶ Place one spoon in the cup of hot water and one in the cup of cold water. Leave the spoons in the cups for a few minutes.

❷ Draw the outline of your partner's hand, palm down, on a sheet of paper.

❸ Dry the hot spoon with the paper towel. Gently touch the back of your partner's hand with the tip of the spoon. Hold it there for one second only. If the spoon feels hot to your partner, mark the spot on your outline with an H.

❹ Heat the spoon again, and repeat the test on your partner's hand 5 mm away from the last spot. Test the entire hand, moving 5 mm at a time. Mark your outline when necessary.

❺ Repeat steps 3 and 4 with the cold spoon. If the spoon feels cold to your partner, mark the spot on your outline with a C.

❻ Trade places with your partner. Repeat steps 1–5.

Interpret your results.

- Each H on your outline shows heat nerve endings, and each C shows cold nerve endings. How close together are the two kinds of nerve endings?

- Do you have the same number of heat nerve endings on your hand as you do cold nerve endings? If not, which do you have more of?

- Do you think you would get the same results if you tested the inner side of your forearm? **Try it!**

Closer to Home:
Reading by touch

Suppose you had a nickel and a quarter in your pocket, and you needed the quarter. Could you take the right coin out without looking? **Try it!** You'll probably use the part of your hand that has the most touch nerve endings.

Some people depend on their sense of touch to read. Have you ever seen the patterns of raised dots next to elevator buttons? The dots may not mean much to you, but a blind person can read them—they are the floor numbers, written in braille. This system of writing was invented in 1824 by a blind 15-year-old French boy named Louis Braille. People read braille by running their fingertips along the raised dots. Words are spelled in braille letters that match the letters of the alphabet people who can see use. Sentences and paragraphs in braille books are set up the same way as in other books.

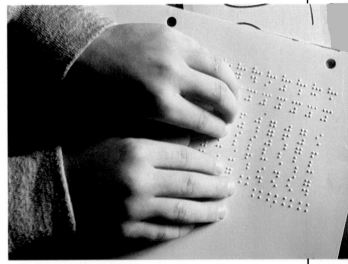

▲ An experienced braille reader can read just as fast as you can.

• In what ways do you "read" with your fingertips?

• What does this braille message say?

THE BRAILLE ALPHABET

A	B	C	D	E	F	G	H	I	J

K	L	M	N	O	P	Q	R	S	T

U	V	W	X	Y	Z	and	for	the	with

Think!

What would happen if you didn't have nerve endings for pain? Would you be better off, or do you think it's important to be able to feel pain? Explain.

What Does Your Brain Do?

As you read this page, your brain gets signals from your eyes. When the signals reach the vision center, you see the words. But signals also go to other parts of the brain, and then you recognize the words that you see and know what they mean. Your brain will store the ideas in your memory. And your brain will send out signals to your muscles that will cause them to turn the page when you've finished reading it.

Your brain is in charge of your body. It gets nearly all the information and it makes nearly all the decisions. Your brain is protected by your skull. It floats in your skull in a clear liquid, which also helps protect it.

The three main parts of your brain are the cerebrum, the cerebellum, and the brain stem. Your cerebrum is the biggest part of your brain. It's the part of your brain that receives signals from your sense organs and changes them into a sense—such as sight or smell. All of your thinking goes on in your cerebrum. Your cerebrum is where decisions are made, including deciding to move your hand or another part of your body. The cerebrum is where your memory is, too. When you're in school, your cerebrum is hard at work—you use it for reading, writing, and speaking.

Even though your cerebrum causes your muscles to move when you do something, your cerebellum helps you control their movement. Think about the different muscles—from your toes to your hips—that you use when you walk. Your cerebellum makes sure that they work together and in the right order. It also helps you keep your balance.

Your spinal cord is connected to your brain stem. Signals to and from the rest of your brain pass through your brain stem. But many signals also start in the brain stem. That's because it controls many of the things that you do without thinking, like breathing, swallowing, and coughing. Your brain stem even controls how fast your heart beats. Most of the time your brain stem does its work without your knowing it.

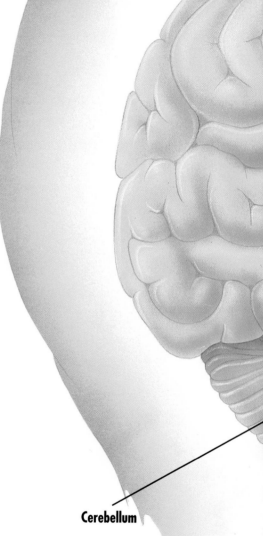

Cerebellum

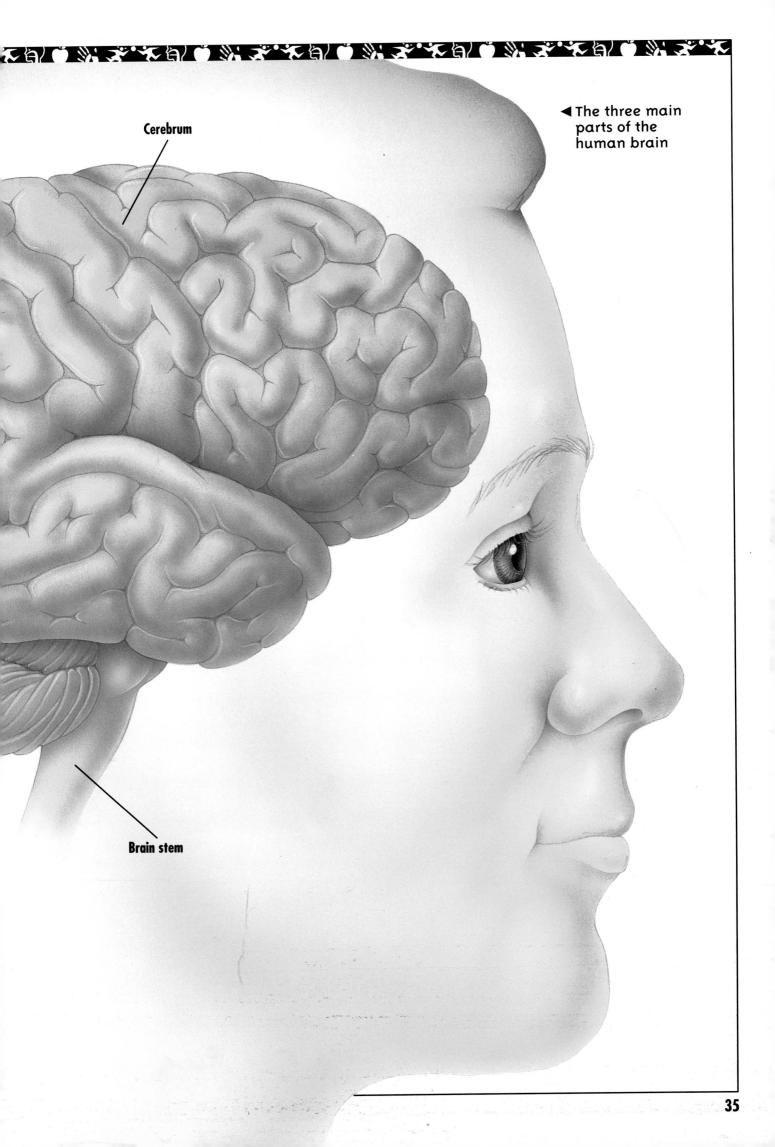

Cerebrum

Brain stem

◄ The three main parts of the human brain

Information Connection:
Using reference books

Just as you've mapped your tongue and hands, doctors have mapped the cerebrum. Different parts of the cerebrum handle different jobs for the body.

You can see that the cerebrum has two different parts for speech. One part controls what words you want to say. The other controls the movement of the muscles you have to use to say the words. Nearly everything you do uses many parts of your brain.

What are some of the parts of your cerebrum you might use for each of the following activities?

- lifting a cup to take a drink

- singing

- hitting a baseball

Which side of your cerebrum would send out a signal that would cause your right hand to move? You can find out by looking at pages 24–25 of *Learning a Lesson*.

▼ This map of the human brain shows some centers for the senses and for movements.

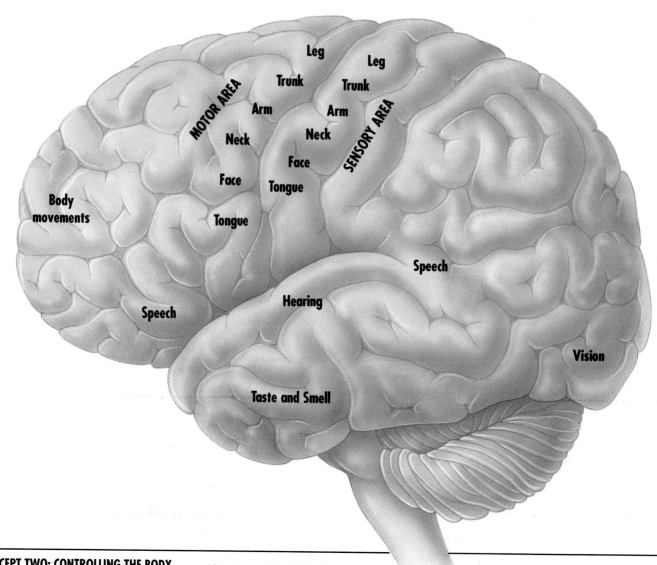

◄ Do you think this batter is left-handed or right-handed?

Closer to Home:
Are you right-eyed or left-eyed?

Your brain decides how you see. Your eyes are a few centimeters apart, so each eye sees from a slightly different position. Your brain prefers one view to the other. You can find out which eye your brain pays the most attention to. **Try it!** Hold up a finger at arm's length, and move the finger until it's directly in line with an object on the other side of the room. Now close your left eye. Did the object seem to move? Which way? Close your right eye. Did the object seem to move?

If the object doesn't move when your right eye is closed, then you're left-eyed. If the object doesn't move when your left eye is closed, you're right-eyed. Right-eyed people can be left-handed, and left-eyed people can be right-handed.

Sometimes the signals from one eye are much weaker than the signals from the other eye. In time, this eye can lose its ability to see. This condition is called lazy eye or amblyopia. It's quite common in children. It's often treated by wearing a patch over the stronger eye. This strengthens the weaker eye so it can send stronger signals to the brain. Lazy eye can also be corrected by exercising the eye muscles or by surgery.

• Some people think it's helpful for a batter in baseball to be left-eyed and right-handed, or right-eyed and left-handed. Why might they think that?

• Some people are right-handed but left-footed. How could you find out if you are one of them?

Think!

Which part of your brain do you think controls your body temperature?

What Are Reflexes?

You know your brain controls your movements by sending signals to your muscles. You found out in Lesson 3 that these signals travel very fast. But there are times when you need to move especially fast. Suppose you're walking barefoot on the grass and suddenly you step on a sharp stone. What's the next move you make? How quickly do you make it? Was your brain in charge?

Exploration:
Test your reflexes.

You need:

Clear plastic wrap
2 rulers
Tape
Cotton ball

❶ Tear off a piece of plastic wrap about 60 cm long. Tape each end to a ruler.

❷ Hold the rulers apart so that the plastic wrap is stretched tight. Use the plastic as a shield for your face. Hold the shield about 22 cm in front of your face.

❸ Have your partner stand between 1 and 2 m away from you and throw the cotton ball at your nose. Record your reactions.

❹ Repeat the activity a few times.

❺ Trade places with your partner. Repeat steps 2–4.

Interpret your results.

• What did you do when the cotton ball was thrown at you?

• Did you do the same thing each time the cotton ball was thrown?

• Did you plan to take this action?

• Do you think you could force yourself not to act this way when the cotton ball is thrown at you? **Try it!**

• Why do you think you act this way when something is thrown at you?

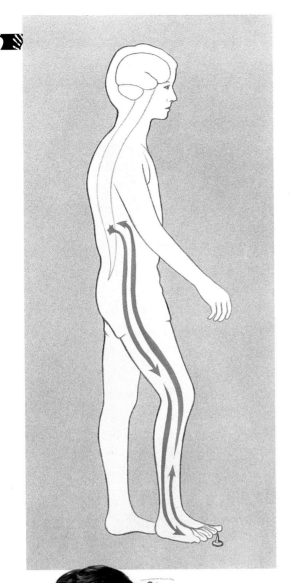
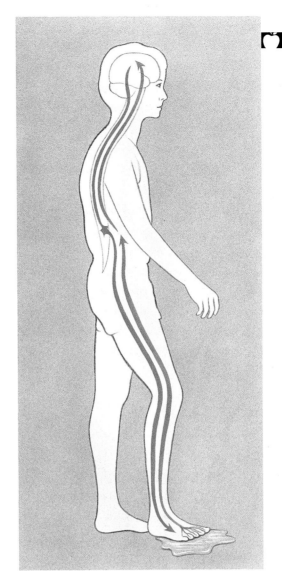

▲ One of these reactions is a reflex action. When the signal from the foot reaches the spinal cord, a signal immediately goes to muscles that move the foot.

Exploration Connection:
Interpreting diagrams

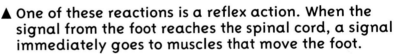 The diagrams show two different paths that signals can take when you make your foot move. One path might be used when your bare toes feel wet grass and you pull your foot back. The other path might be used when you step on a sharp stone. Compare the diagrams. What differences can you find between the two paths?

Reflex actions are one of the ways your body protects itself. When you step on something sharp, your foot moves away before you even feel pain. This is a reflex action. Reflex actions are the quickest reactions your body can have because the signals that cause them follow a shortcut. Can you see the shortcut they use in the diagram? When you step on something sharp, why do you think you don't feel pain until after you've moved your foot?

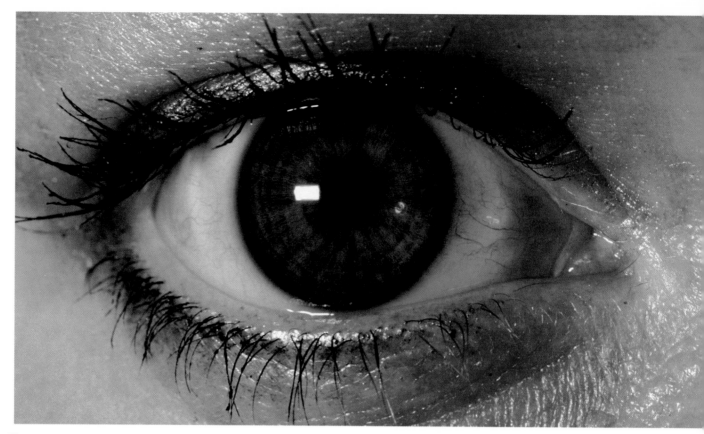

Closer to Home: Everyday reflexes

Has a doctor ever tapped your leg just below the knee with a small rubber hammer? What did you do? Do you think you could have made yourself not do it? The doctor was testing one of your reflexes. Here's a reflex you can test yourself. Think of something delicious to eat. What happens? **Try it!** Does everybody react to the thought of food in the same way?

Your everyday life involves many reflex actions. Some of them seem so common that you probably haven't thought about what causes them. Sneezes and hiccups are reflex actions. So are coughs. Can you think of any others?

You don't have to learn most reflex actions the way you have to learn how to walk. From the moment you were born, your nerve cells sent signals over shortcuts. Many reflexes, such as blinking, protect you. Many others keep your body working properly.

▲ When the pupil of your eye gets smaller in bright light, is it a reflex action? Why or why not?

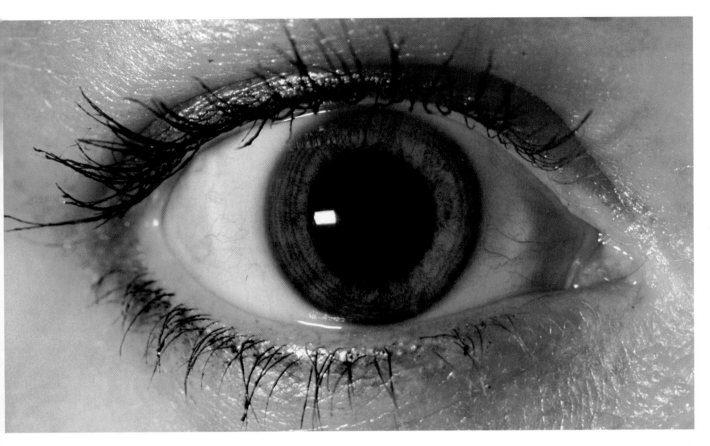

For instance, when you take a bite of food, a reflex causes saliva to flow into your mouth. The saliva mixes with your food, helping to digest it and making it easier to swallow.

You also carry out some reflex actions you weren't born with—you developed them as you grew older. That's why your mouth waters when you smell food you especially like. You've learned that certain odors mean favorite foods are nearby. Now nerve cells in your mouth react to the smell of food just as they do when you're actually eating.

What do you do when someone yells "Catch!" and throws a ball at you? Do you think this is a reflex action? Could you choose not to react that way? Your reaction is one you learned—you weren't born knowing how to react that way. Do you think you react to the shout "Catch!" or to the ball heading in your direction? **Try it!**

◀ Even if you break a balloon yourself, you'll show some reflex actions.

It's not easy, but you can learn to control some reflexes, even the kind you were born with. Remember the reflex you investigated in the Exploration? With hard work and long hours of training, baseball catchers are able to stop themselves from reacting this way. Why do you think they want to control this reflex?

• Why is sneezing a reflex action?

• Suppose you're walking on an icy sidewalk and your feet start to slip. What reflex actions do you take?

When you hear a sudden, very loud clap of thunder, what actions do you take? Which of them do you think are reflex actions?

What Is Your Memory?

Do you remember what you did in Exploration 10 to test your reflexes? Try to answer without looking back. How do you know what you did yesterday, or even a year ago? Your brain contains more facts than you could begin to count. Just think about what you know about some of your friends: their names, phone numbers, birthdays, favorite music, and so on. You probably even know the colors of their backpacks.

Exploration:
Name that face.

You need:

ThinkMat 11
Scissors
Pencil
Clock or watch

❶ Cut along the dotted lines of the ThinkMat to make two strips of paper. Save them.

❷ Under each face on the ThinkMat, write a different name. Each name should be simple, such as George Garcia or Jenny Smith. (Don't let your partner see what you write.)

❸ Have your partner study the ThinkMat for 15 seconds.

❹ Cover the names with the strips of paper. Your partner will try to remember the name that goes with each face. Record the number of correct matches.

❺ Let your partner study the ThinkMat for 60 seconds, and repeat step 4.

❻ Trade places with your partner. Work with a new ThinkMat, and repeat steps 1–5.

Interpret your results.

- How many correct matches did you make after studying the ThinkMat for 15 seconds? for 60 seconds?

- Do you think you'd make more correct matches if you studied the ThinkMat for two minutes?

- How many correct matches could you make tomorrow without first studying? **Try it!**

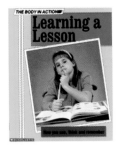

Exploration Connection:
Using reference books

When you store facts in your brain, the facts become part of your memory. If you need to or want to, you can get the facts out of storage. What do you call it when you get facts out of your memory? Which part of your brain do you think controls your memory? You can find out by reading pages 18–19 of *Learning a Lesson*.

You have short-term memory and long-term memory. Short-term memory holds information for only a few seconds or minutes. Then you either lose the information or it's stored in long-term memory. Long-term memory holds huge amounts of information. Some you will remember for a day, some for a week or a month. Some you will remember for the rest of your life. Which kind of memory would you use when you look up a phone number and remember it long enough to dial it? Which would you use when you learn a song?

Closer to Home: Mnemonics

You need to remember a lot of information to get through a day. Luckily, there are ways to help you to remember, such as mnemonics. (The word rhymes with "the Sonics," and you don't pronounce the *m*.) Mnemonics can help you remember important things.

Here's one example of a mnemonic. The names of the five Great Lakes are Huron, Ontario, Michigan, Erie, and Superior. Write down the first letter of each name. What word do the letters form? This word is a mnemonic that many people use to remember the names of the Great Lakes.

You might know the names of the planets in the solar system. They are Earth, Jupiter, Mars, Uranus, Pluto, Venus, Mercury, Neptune, and Saturn. Here's a mnemonic to help you remember the order of the planets from the sun: My very eager mother just served us nine pizzas. Can you figure out how the mnemonic works?

Any tricks that you use to remember things are mnemonics. You can even use them for math. Lots of people use a simple trick to multiply by 9. Here's how it works. Place your hands palm down in front of you. Suppose you want to know what 3 times 9 is. Bend your third finger from the far left. The fingers to the left of it are tens, the ones to the right are ones. How can you use this mnemonic to find 8 times 9? **Try it!**

- Why would a bank list its phone number as 1-800-THE-BANK? What would the phone number be in numbers?

- What's an easy way to remember the phone number 910-1112?

- What word can you think up as a mnemonic for your own phone number or for a friend's phone number? **Try it!**

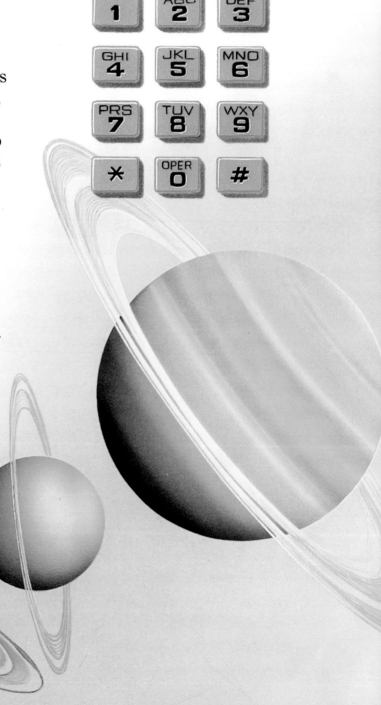

3 x 9 = 27

2 tens

7 ones

MULTIPLYING BY 9

Think!

Because of disease or injury, some people can't add new information to their long-term memory. How could this affect their lives?

How Does Your Brain Use Experience to Interpret Signals?

You use your memory for simple things like remembering your own name. You also use it to remember more complicated things like the order of the planets. You're even using memory right now. If you had no memory, could you read this question? Do you think you can look at a word and not read it? Try to look at the word below without reading it.

lunch

Exploration:
Identify a picture.

❶ Look at the shape below. Record what you think it is.

❷ Now turn the book so that the page numbers are at the top. Look at the drawing again and record what you think it is now.

❸ Look at the drawing below on the right. Which of the logs is longer? Measure them.

Interpret your results.

• What did you see in step 1? What did you see when you turned the page upside down?

• If you saw this shape upside down many times, do you think you would know what it is after a time? Why?

• Were you correct about the logs in step 3? Why do you think you answered the way you did?

• How does experience affect the way your brain understands signals?

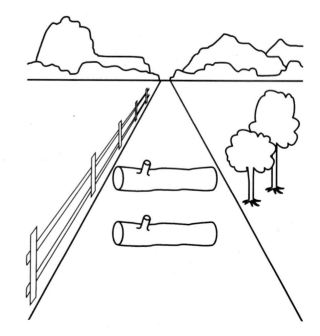

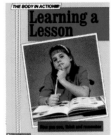

Exploration Connection: Using reference books

Sometimes your sense organs send signals to the brain that aren't familiar. Your brain searches its experience to try to understand the signals. Look at the painting by Pablo Picasso on the left. You've never seen anything exactly like the painting, but you can probably figure out what it shows. How do you think your brain made sense of the painting?

Picasso used geometric shapes or cubes to show what he was painting. This painting style is called cubism. The other picture, by Paul Signac, is painted in a style called pointillism. How do you think this style got its name? If you hold the book close to your face, can you tell what's in the picture? **Try it!** Now look at the picture from far away. What does your brain do to help you understand the picture? You can find out more about how the brain helps to make sense out of unfamiliar things by reading pages 17 and 20–22 of *Learning a Lesson.*

◄ This is a detail from the large painting below. Where does it fit?

► This is a detail from the large painting above. Where does it fit?

Giraudon/Art Resource/NY. Paul Signac, "The Port of Saint Tropez"

You managed to understand the painting by Pablo Picasso. Suppose you'd seen only the bottom half of the painting. Would it have made any sense to you? You need experience to understand many of the signals your brain receives. But sometimes you can be misled by your experience.

Exploration:
Question what you see.

You need:
Ruler
Pencil

❶ Look at the word THIEF. Are the letters complete? Record your observation. ✏

❷ Look at lines A and B. Which line is longer? Record your observation. ✏

❸ Look at the black and white pattern. Are the rows of squares across the pattern straight or slanted? Record your observation. ✏

Interpret your results.

• Did you think that the word THIEF was written in complete letters? Why or why not? Move your finger along the lines of each letter to see if you were correct.

• Which line did you think was longer: A or B? Use your ruler to see if you were right.

• Did you think that the rows across the pattern were slanted? If so, what made you think that? Use your ruler to find out if you were correct.

• How does experience sometimes mislead you when you look at something?

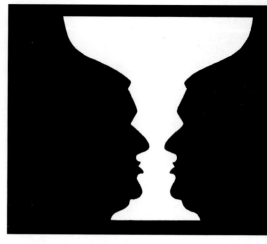

▲ Do you see a vase or two faces?

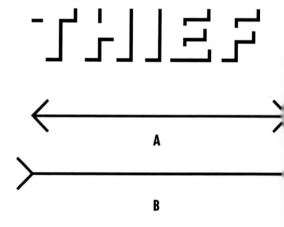

Closer to Home:
Reading faces

Using your own experience, you learned to read faces long before you could talk. When you were just a tiny baby, you began to know the difference between a smile and a frown. A smile could make you smile, too. How do you think you responded to a frown? Today you probably use your knowledge of what a person's expression means whenever you see someone.

People aren't the only ones who have feelings. If you know what clues to look for, you can often read a dog's face. Which of the dogs on this page would you avoid?

- How do you think you learned what a frown or a smile meant?

- Some people think they can tell what another person is feeling by looking at his or her eyes. What do you think? Why?

- Do you think a dog trainer can read a dog's face more easily than you can? Why?

▲ Is this really moving?

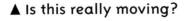
Think!

Is what you've learned from experience stored in your short-term memory or long-term memory? Why do you think so?

How Can You Protect Your Nervous System?

You can use your experience to avoid things that you know might be dangerous. And your reflex actions can help protect you when something unexpected happens.

All the parts of your nervous system are very important to you. They are also among the most difficult parts to repair—even with the help of doctors. What are some ways you can protect your nervous system?

Exploration:
Observe the ways people protect their nervous systems.

❶ For one full day, observe the ways people protect their nervous systems. How do they protect the head, spinal cord, and sense organs? Pay attention to things they wear, special equipment they use, and even the way they do things.

❷ Record your observations. Try to find things to list in all four columns of the LabMat.

Interpret your results.

• How were the ways people protect their nervous systems alike in each column of the LabMat? How were they different?

• Which parts of their nervous systems did the people you observed protect most often? Why do you think that was so?

• Do you know of other ways that people protect their nervous systems? Add them to the LabMat.

▶ The government requires construction workers to wear hardhats.

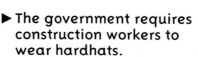

Exploration Connection:
Interpreting tables

When you did the Exploration, did you notice the ways that people protect their hearing? Loud noise can damage a person's hearing. Loudness is measured in decibels—a unit named after Alexander Graham Bell, the scientist who invented the telephone.

Listening to sounds above 90 decibels for a long time every day can damage hearing.

People who work with or around noisy equipment should wear ear protectors to prevent this damage. Sounds louder than about 130 decibels cause pain, and sounds louder than 160 decibels can cause deafness. What sounds do you think might cause deafness? Name some work you think people should do only when they're wearing ear protectors.

Sound	Loudness In Decibels
A whisper	20
The sounds in an average home	50
Normal conversation	65
Vacuum cleaner	80
Police siren	95
Chain saw	115
Loud thunder	120
Jet plane taking off	140

▲ Why does this person wear ear protectors?

Closer to Home: Biking safely

If you think about all the things you do and everything that goes on inside you, you may wonder how the brain can control and oversee so much activity. The brain's amazing powers are all due to its nerve cells—more than 100 billion of them are packed in the brain. Is that number mind boggling to you? This comparison may give you a better feeling for what 100 billion means. Suppose you had 100 billion dollars and wanted to get rid of every penny within 50 years. To reach your goal, you'd have to spend between 5 million and 6 million dollars *every day* for the next 50 years.

That's a lot of brain cells—and they're a part of one of the softest, most delicate tissues of the body. Fortunately, the brain has lots of protection inside your skull. The brain is housed inside the cranium, the top part of the skull. It's one of the strongest parts of your body. The rest of the skull supports the brain and keeps it from bouncing around inside the cranium.

Your skull protects your brain from everyday bumps and bangs. But skulls weren't made for high-speed crashes. That's why you'll hardly ever see a serious bicycle rider without a helmet. Many towns, counties, and states have passed laws that require children to wear helmets when they bike.

Soft foam pads

Hard foam
The inner layer is made of a hard foam to absorb the force of a bang against the helmet.

Vent hole
The vent holes help keep your head cool as you ride.

Hard plastic shell
The outer cover of the helmet is hard plastic.

Chin strap

Most bike helmets weigh about as much as a loaf of bread. Even though helmets aren't very heavy, they can provide a lot of protection—and bike riders need protection! Experts say that 20 out of every 100 children who ride bikes have bike accidents, and 3 out of those 20 children receive head injuries in their accidents.

- If you have a bad accident, the outer cover of the helmet may get cracked or crushed. Why does the helmet still protect your skull?

- Why do you think bike helmets are often made in bright colors?

- Some people don't wear bike helmets because they don't like the way the helmets look. Is this a good reason not to wear a bike helmet? Explain.

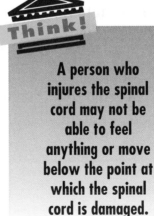

Think!

A person who injures the spinal cord may not be able to feel anything or move below the point at which the spinal cord is damaged. Why?

How Can You Keep Your Nervous System Healthy?

You've thought about ways to protect your nervous system from harm. There are other important things you can do to help your nervous system. Keeping yourself healthy is one of them. There are also some particular things that help your nervous system remain healthy. For example, your eyes need Vitamin A and your nervous system needs B vitamins to work properly.

It's important for you to get shots from a doctor to protect you against diseases. Some diseases attack the nervous system. Tetanus, which you can get from an infected cut, affects the nervous system. Some diseases such as mumps and measles can attack your nervous system if they aren't treated right away. Shots can give protection against these diseases.

Your nervous system works hard, and it needs to rest. When you sleep, your body—including your nervous system—repairs itself. When you don't get enough sleep, it affects how your nervous system works the next day. You don't think as clearly and it's harder to pay attention to what you're doing. Some scientists think that sleep helps our brains to organize memories.

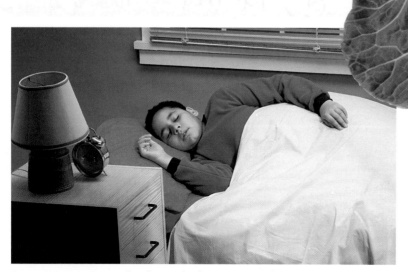

▲ Getting enough sleep helps your nervous system to do its work.

Information Connection:
Interpreting tables

You might think that when you fall asleep your sleep gets deeper and deeper until it's time to wake up. But that isn't what happens. Your sleep gets deeper and then lighter several times during the night. Periods of light sleep are often interrupted by a period of rapid eye movement sleep, or REM for short. You are in REM sleep three to five times each night. Scientists believe that you dream during REM sleep and that it helps you learn, think, and feel. Which part of the brain do you think needs REM sleep? What is the total amount of REM sleep shown on the table?

▼ The orange blocks show periods of one person's REM sleep.

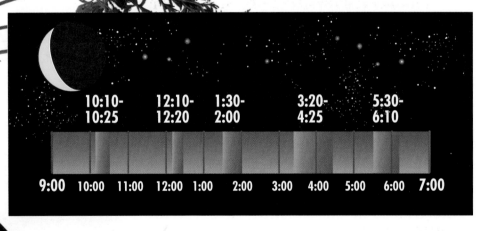

| 10:10–10:25 | 12:10–12:20 | 1:30–2:00 | 3:20–4:25 | 5:30–6:10 |
| 9:00 | 10:00 | 11:00 | 12:00 | 1:00 | 2:00 | 3:00 | 4:00 | 5:00 | 6:00 | 7:00 |

◄ Green, leafy vegetables can give you important B vitamins, and carrots and sweet potatoes provide Vitamin A.

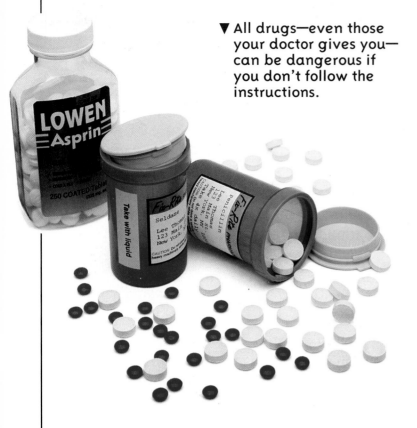

▼ All drugs—even those your doctor gives you— can be dangerous if you don't follow the instructions.

Closer to Home: The dangers of drug abuse

Your nervous system does an amazing job. It even produces chemicals that can stop you from feeling pain, or make you feel very happy. Have you noticed that when you cut yourself, the pain slowly goes away? Or when you have exercised hard, you feel extra glad?

Sometimes when you have pain, the brain's chemicals may not stop you from feeling it. A doctor might give you a medicine to do this job. Medicines—even the kinds you can buy without a doctor's prescription—are drugs. Any chemical that changes how your body works is a drug.

Many drugs are useful. Antibiotics can kill bacteria that make you sick. These drugs save lives. Many other drugs can make the body work properly when it can't do so by itself. For example, people whose hearts don't beat properly can be helped by drugs.

Some drugs work directly on the nervous system. Painkillers do, and so do drugs that help people who have mental illnesses.

When you take a drug, it's important to use it correctly. Then the drug can do the job it's meant to do, and you'll feel better sooner. Using a drug correctly means that you follow your doctor's instructions or those printed on the package the drug comes in. You have to take the right amount of drug at the proper times.

Some chemicals that change the way the body works are drugs, but they're not used as medicines. One of these drugs is alcohol, which affects the nervous system. Many adults drink small amounts of alcohol. But this drug is very dangerous for children and teenagers. Alcohol interferes with the normal development of young people.

Some people drink a lot of alcohol. Too much alcohol in the body slows down the working of the nervous system. People who drink too much alcohol may get angry or sad. They may fall asleep. If they drink too much alcohol all the time, they may not be able to stop drinking without getting sick. That's because their bodies have become dependent on alcohol. Their bodies can't work properly without it. This is called addiction.

Some kinds of dangerous drugs

STIMULANTS such as "speed," cocaine,"crack"	These drugs speed up the brain. Extended us or an overdose can cause death. Addictive.
DEPRESSANTS such as alcohol, sleeping pills	These drugs slow down and interfere with messages to and from the brain. Extended u or an overdose can cause death. Addictive.
NARCOTICS such as heroin	These drugs change a person's mood and slo down messages to and from the brain. Exten use or an overdose can cause death. Addict
HALLUCINOGENS such as LSD, marijuana	These drugs change the way people see, hear, and feel things around them. This can be a terrifying experience.

▲ When you get exercise, your brain makes chemicals that make you feel good.

Two more drugs that change the way the nervous system works are cocaine and heroin. It's against the law to take these drugs, but some people do. They use drugs to trick their brains into making them feel good. That works for a time, but soon their brains make less of the natural chemicals that make people feel good. Then the people who take these drugs are addicted to them. They depend on the drugs to feel well, and they get sick without them.

But addiction isn't the only danger of drug abuse. Drugs have other effects on the nervous system. Some drugs, such as alcohol, can cause people to become clumsy and to think less clearly. Other drugs, such as cocaine, make people restless, scared of people, and bad-tempered. Drugs that affect your nervous system can change the way

you think and change your judgment. Using dangerous drugs can also damage other parts of your body, such as your lungs, heart, liver, and kidneys.

- Why is it dangerous when someone drives after they have been drinking alcohol?

- How might drug abusers affect other people's lives?

- Are all dangerous drugs illegal? Explain.

Think!

You have slept for a total of about three years. Was it a waste of time? Explain.

Identify Problems: Designing a Robot

Think Tank Road Map

One day humans may not only travel from planet to planet, but might even live somewhere other than Earth.

For years NASA scientists have had their eyes on Mars as the site for a future human outpost. But can people really live there? Even though the *Viking* landers sent back hundreds of pictures and conducted many tests, they couldn't tell us if a human could live on Mars. So NASA has asked you and your team of robot specialists for help.

15 • In Lesson 15 you're going to identify the problems you'd have to solve to build a special kind of robot.

16 • In Lesson 16 you'll find some possible solutions to these problems.

17 • In Lesson 17 you'll design the robot and make a model of your design.

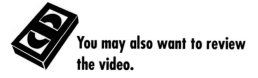
You may also want to review the video.

Problem: NASA is making plans to build a scientific outpost on Mars. You and your team have been hired to design a robot that will react to the Martian environment much like humans would.

↓ These questions will help you make a list of the problems you'll face while trying to design your robot.

1 What have you already learned about the ways you get information about the environment? What kinds of things do your senses tell you about the world? What would you want to know about the environment on Mars?

2 A robot is a machine that can do some of the things people can do. People gather information through their senses. What kinds of devices would a robot need in order to gather information?

3 What will the robot look like? How will it get around?

4 The robot will be all alone on Mars. How will it take care of itself in an emergency? What will happen if it falls or if a part breaks?

5 Machines that can imitate some of the things people do are more common than you may think. Here are three examples. As you study the pictures, ask yourself: What kinds of problems did the designers face in trying to get their machines to imitate a human?

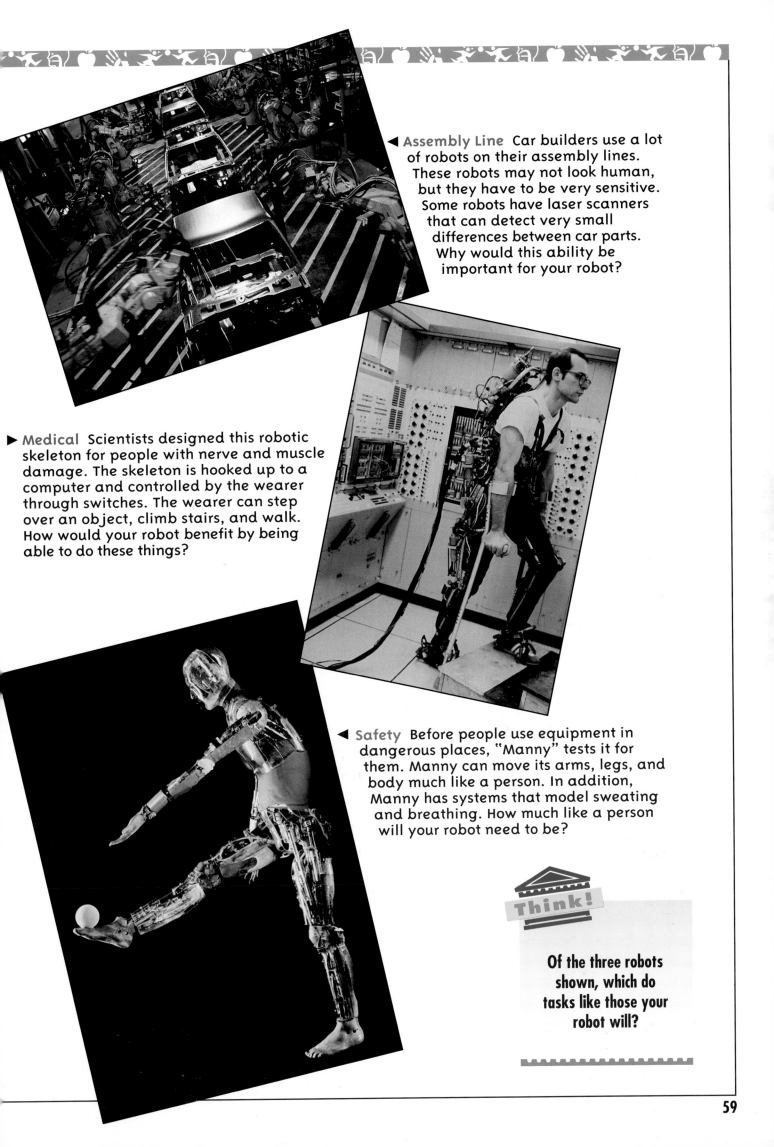

◀ **Assembly Line** Car builders use a lot of robots on their assembly lines. These robots may not look human, but they have to be very sensitive. Some robots have laser scanners that can detect very small differences between car parts. Why would this ability be important for your robot?

▶ **Medical** Scientists designed this robotic skeleton for people with nerve and muscle damage. The skeleton is hooked up to a computer and controlled by the wearer through switches. The wearer can step over an object, climb stairs, and walk. How would your robot benefit by being able to do these things?

◀ **Safety** Before people use equipment in dangerous places, "Manny" tests it for them. Manny can move its arms, legs, and body much like a person. In addition, Manny has systems that model sweating and breathing. How much like a person will your robot need to be?

Think!

Of the three robots shown, which do tasks like those your robot will?

Find Solutions: Designing a Robot

You've just identified some problems robot designers faced. Now you'll see how some designers have solved the problem of trying to make their robots respond to their environment the way a human being would. Studying their solutions might help you put together your robot.

Robots, androids, and cyborgs: fact or fiction?

What's the difference between a robot, an android, and a cyborg? Where does fact end and fiction begin? The term *robot* was invented in 1917 by the Czechoslovakian writer Karel Capek. A robot is a machine that may or may not look human but can perform human tasks.

Android comes from two Greek words meaning "of man" and "form." An android is a machine that has biological parts like organs and skin. Androids are, of course, still science fiction.

A cyborg, which is also science fiction, is a human with a lot of machine parts that give the cyborg "superhuman" abilities.

1

Make a chart of the problems you listed in the last lesson. Beside each of your problems, try to list a similar problem that these robots' designers faced. Then list the ways that your robot has to be different.

2

The pictures on these pages show how robot designers have handled individual problems. Study their solutions.

3

Notice the special task that each robot is able to perform. How do the robots' systems imitate the way the human nervous system works? Will any of those solutions help you in designing your robot?

4

Below each problem you listed in your chart for building a robot, record any solutions you can think of. If you have more than one solution to a problem, record them all. You may want to use words and pictures.

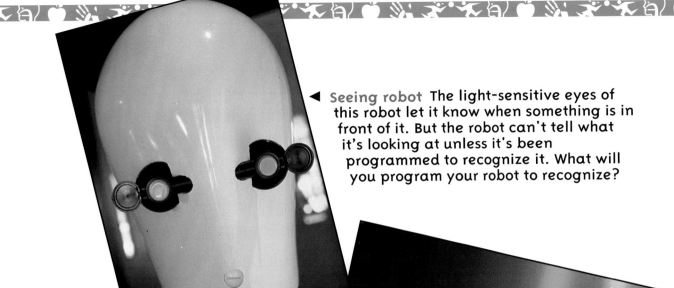

◄ **Seeing robot** The light-sensitive eyes of this robot let it know when something is in front of it. But the robot can't tell what it's looking at unless it's been programmed to recognize it. What will you program your robot to recognize?

► **Grasping robot** The metal arms and hands of this robot can be adjusted to handle small objects. What will your robot need to be able to pick up?

◄ **Walking robot** This spiderlike robot can change the length of each of its legs so it can walk on uneven surfaces. What types of surfaces will your robot need to walk on?

Other resources you can check:

• To find out more about how robots work: *Robots: Your High-tech World,* by Gloria Skurzynski. Bradbury Press, 1990.

• To find out more about your nervous system: *Come to Your Senses (All Eleven of Them),* by Milan Tytla. Annick Press, 1993.

How can looking at the design of other robots help you to design your robot?

Make Models: Designing a Robot

Your team has identified problems and solutions you'll face in building a robot that responds to its environment the way a human would. Now you can make a model based on those solutions.

Possible models for your robot:

Diagram Use the diagrams in Lessons 1–14 to help you draw diagrams of the working parts of your robot. Be sure to label your diagram to show your solutions.

Written Description Write a report that carefully describes every detail of your robot: its parts, its size, and its materials.

Computer Graphics Use a graphics program to design your Mars robot on a computer.

Oral Presentation Give a speech about your robot as if your team were making a presentation to NASA.

3-Dimensional Model Use cardboard, wire, or any combination of materials to build the frame of your robot. Include labels describing how each part would work.

1 Mars is about 50 million miles farther from the sun than Earth is. In what ways is building a robot for Mars different from building one for Earth?

2 Work with your team to design a Mars robot. List all the features your robot should have so it can respond to its environment the way a human might.

3 Make a model based on your design. Choose one of the models shown on this page.

4 Look at all the models your class has made. How did different teams solve different problems?

5 What did you learn in this unit that helped you design your robot?

Surface of Mars

Resources for designing your robot:

• For information you've collected about the senses, the brain, and the nervous system, check your journals and LabMats from the first part of this unit.

• The graphics and information in this unit will help you design your robot.

• The reference books from this unit are filled with information on how we process information about our environment.

• Refer to the Video Clue Log. What characteristics of the nervous system did the Science Sleuths investigate?

• Interview other teams to find out how they may have solved problems that are giving you trouble.

Think!

As you made the model of your robot, what other problems and solutions did you think of?

FOR SCIENCE BROWSERS

All articles reprinted with permission.

Do Animals See TV the Way We Do?

from *Ranger Rick*

Some do and some don't. To understand why, you have to know something about how TV works.

A TV screen shows lots of still pictures, one after another. In fact, it shows about 60 different still pictures every second. As people watch these pictures, their eyes and brains are fooled into seeing the different pictures as one moving picture.

Many animals, such as dragonflies, aren't so easy to fool. Their eyes and brains work much faster than people's. That means they see each of the TV's still pictures one at a time. They see the pictures, but they don't see any movement.

For these animals' eyes and brains to be fooled into seeing movement, the TV screen would have to show the pictures much, much faster.

But some other animals, such as chickens, chimps, cats, jumping spiders, and possibly dogs, would make great couch potatoes. Their eyes and brains can be fooled just as people's are, so they can see the action on a TV screen.

—*February, 1993*

It's Okay to Laugh, It's Okay to Cry

by Peggy Noll
from *Highlights*

Your laughing and crying are two signs that you are a human being. Today medical scientists are saying also that laughing and crying are good for you.

It's OK to cry.

No one likes to be called a "crybaby." But it seems people need to cry, at least sometimes. There are really three different kinds of tears:

1) the ones that keep your eyes moist all the time,

2) the ones that come when you get dust in your eye or smell a strong onion,

3) the ones that come when you are especially sad—or happy!

It is only that third kind of tear that is special to humans.

It's also called "emotional crying" and is the subject of a book called *Crying: The Mystery of Tears.*

Before the author, Dr. William H. Frey, could study tears, he first had to collect them. He ran an ad in the newspaper that read "Will you cry for me?"

Lots of people said they would. As volunteers in Dr. Frey's project, they sat in an auditorium and watched sad movies. They held test tubes just below their eyelids to collect their tears.

Dr. Frey decided that many people need to learn that it is OK to cry. "They do not have to be strong all the time," he said.

Laughter is a lot like tears.

Crying and laughing are really more alike than they are different. Both may be important to good health.

Norman Cousins, a well-known editor, was one of the first in recent years to write about the power of laughter. Cousins told how he watched Marx Brothers movies and "Candid Camera" reruns when he was recovering from a major illness. He thought that helped him more than pain pills. Cousins surprised many people when he said, "I made the joyous discovery that ten minutes of genuine belly laughter would give me at least two hours of pain-free sleep."

Some scientists agreed with Cousins that laughter is good medicine. Laughing may help release substances in the body that act as natural painkillers. In addition, laughter increases the heart rate and helps breathing and muscle tone.

It seems that sobs and chuckles are both good for you. So when things really get bad, go ahead and cry. But when you hurt all over or need to find a way out of a jam—try laughing.

—*October, 1991*

Color Vision of Cats

Cats can see differences between shades of green, yellow, and blue, but not between shades of yellow and red.

C. Steven Gottlieb/
FPG Int'l. Corp.

UPI/Bettman

He Never Heard the Footsteps

by Jim Murray
excerpt from *Los Angeles Times*

He was the best miler in the world for nine years. He was the world record-holder, also, in the 1,500 meters and in the 800 meters.

He was an elegant runner who had the deceptive kick of Man o' War at the tape. He accelerated without seeming to.

He was a cinch to become the first American to win the Olympic gold medal in the metric mile since 1908.

What nobody knew was Jim Ryun couldn't hear the cheers [or] the gun. Some guys with keen hearing get off the blocks when the hammer clicks. Jim Ryun needed the explosion.

Ryun was born with a hearing impairment. He wasn't deaf. But he could hear only half as well as he should have.

The mile is a race in which hearing can be important, if not critical. The sound of footsteps, the official barking off the splits, the sound of the crowd, all contribute to your pace. Ryun ran it in semisilence.

For years, track and field experts were mystified by Ryun's looking over his shoulder, even in some of his record races. A famous picture of the 1968 Olympics shows him in second place, behind Kip Keino in the 1,500, casting a desperate look so far over his shoulder he is almost turned around and running backward as he tries to see what's coming up behind him.

He wore a wristwatch in all his races, checking it lap by lap. He also would watch the scoreboard clock. He needed visual aids. He raced in a near vacuum.

But Jim Ryun was born to run, and the sound of silence wasn't to keep him from it. At 6 feet 3 and 140 pounds, he was the most graceful at

Fingertip Sense
Your fingers are so sensitive that you can feel a gnat walking on them. One square inch of fingertip skin has about 9,000 nerve endings that sense touch!

his distances since the legendary Mal Whitfield. Other runners ran with face-contorted effort. Ryun ran with the effortless grace of a thoroughbred.

In 1968, he was widely believed to have been the best miler ever. He had qualified for the 1964 Olympics as a teenager—only 17 at the time—and he was to improve annually till he set his first world record in the mile, 3:51.3 in 1966. It was a mark he broke a year later with a 3:51.1. In 1967, he broke the 1,500-meter world record with 3:33.1, a mark that held for five years.

Shortly after that, there was a hearing breakthrough.

"For years, all I heard was, 'There is nothing we can do.' The hearing aids were only somewhat effective. They were merely amplification devices. Then, one day, they brought out a new invention, a programmable hearing device that really lets you hear."

"With these new programmable hearing devices, we can now hear sounds the way everyone hears them," he says. "I'll never forget the day I was standing in a field in Kansas and I heard this sound and I said, 'What's that?' And they said, 'It's the sound of geese flying over.' I was thrilled. I must have been around that sound all my life and never heard it before."

—*May, 1994*

Train Your Brain

by **Nancy Finton**
from *SuperScience Blue*

Can you make your brain stronger by exercising it? Sounds weird, but in fact, you're probably doing it right now. Scientists have discovered that thinking hard may make your brain work better.

Inside your brain are millions of connected nerves. (See below.) These nerves carry lots of information—about what you see and hear, what you remember, and more.

Scientist Bob Jacobs and his team studied the part of the brain that helps us understand language. The team compared brains that had gotten a workout—from people who went to college or had a brain-busting job—with less-active brains.

What did they find? The branches of the nerves in the active brains grew longer than the branches in the others! Longer branches can carry more information. And that means that the brain can do its job better. So make sure your brain gets plenty of exercise this school year—think hard! — *September, 1993*

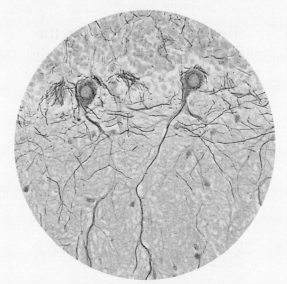

© **Biophoto Associates/Photo Researchers, Inc.**

A Dog's Nose
Part of your nose is lined with nerve cells that sense smells. The same part of a dog's nose is 15 times larger than yours!

Goose Bumps and Nerves
You get goose bumps when you're cold because you're hairy! Tiny hairs that you can see with a hand lens cover your body. The root of each hair grows in a tiny pocket under your skin. That pocket is connected to a tiny muscle. If you get cold, nerves in your skin send signals to your brain. Your brain signals the tiny muscle to tighten up, pulling on the hair. The skin between those tiny muscles becomes bumpy— goose bumpy.

Robots Make Sense

by Lois Markham
from *Kids Discover: The Five Senses*

Ticklish?
Try tickling yourself in your most ticklish spot. It probably won't work. The funny feeling you get when somebody tickles you is an involuntary reflex that happens when the part of your body being tickled is surprised. When you try to tickle yourself, your brain has already warned the area that something's about to happen— so no involuntary reflex happens.

Household robots that respond to human commands have been a dream for years. And modern technology is getting closer to them than ever before. The trick is combining electronic sensors with sophisticated computers.

Robots that see and feel their way around are already a reality. Now researchers at AT&T Bell Laboratories have built a machine with a hearing and speaking vocabulary of 127 words. With those few words, a possible 300 quintillion sensible sentences can be made. A researcher at the Mellon Institute in Pittsburgh is working on a "chemical nose" that could sniff out harmful substances in the air around factories. Others are experimenting with biosensors that could detect toxic gases or measure the sugar content in various foods. They envision a day when food-processing plants will employ roving robots to sample different vats of fruit juices and compare each one to what the robot knows as "good juice."

—October, 1991

Hank Morgan, Science Source/ Photo Researchers, Inc.

Robots with vision (above) avoid obstacles as they deliver meal trays in hospitals. Actually, an electronic camera hooked up to a computer directs the robot.

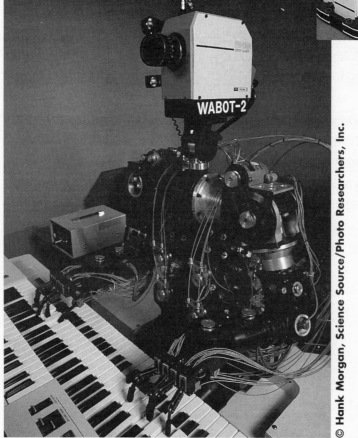

WABOT-2

© Hank Morgan, Science Source/Photo Researchers, Inc.

This piano-playing robot (left) plays requests from the audience.

Employing Good Senses

by Elizabeth Campbell
from *MAINSTREAM, Magazine of the Able-Disabled*

Tony Record

The ticking of several hundred clocks sounded like falling raindrops as I stepped inside the turn-of-the-century building. The musty smell of the old building filled the air as the owner of a resident antique shop described its eclectic collection of furniture and other mementos from the past.

Later, as water lapped against a dock, I stood on the upper deck of a paddle-wheel riverboat listening to members of the crew talk about cruises people can take on Lake Granbury.

Exploring the antique shop and the riverboat in the north central Texas town of Granbury were just two of the experiences I had during a recent visit to the town to write a story to tell newspaper readers what they can do and see during a weekend visit.

The people of Granbury were wonderfully descriptive of their town. They really helped me see and feel it, so that I could make my readers see it, too.

As a blind person working as a writer at the Fort Worth Star-Telegram, I don't gather information visually. I ask people I am with to describe visual elements such as the colors of a room or what types of paintings are on the walls. I use the other senses such as hearing and smell in my descriptions.

This has helped me write about exhibits at local museums, a Fort Worth realtor who takes food and clothing to Mexico and cosmonauts visiting from the former Soviet Union. And I write about weekend travel. Every Saturday, people can turn to the Life section and read about area festivals. I travel to nearby towns to describe attractions such as unusual bed and breakfasts, museums and historic homes.

Like everyone else, I do many of my interviews over the telephone, but I also get out of the office for assignments. I either take taxis or ride with photographers.

I was hired on a nine-week trial basis because the management had no experience with a blind reporter. I never thought that my blindness hindered me from doing interviews or writing stories and I knew that I had the skills to do the job. Once I showed them that I had the necessary skills and competence to do the job, I was hired full-time.
— *October, 1992*

The Blinking Reflex

Try to stop blinking for 60 seconds. Can you do it? Most humans blink automatically every 2 to 10 seconds. It's a reflex action that causes tears to bathe your eyes, keeping them clean and moist.

Concept vocabulary and other technical terms

blind spot [blīnd spot]: *n.* The place in the retina with no nerve cells that react to light; this is where the retina connects with the seeing nerve.

brain [brān]: *n.* The control center of the nervous system.

brain stem [brān stem]: *n.* The part of the brain that connects with the spinal cord; it controls heartbeat, breathing, and other automatic body actions .

cerebellum [ser·ə·bel'·əm]: *n.* The part of the brain that helps muscles work together and controls balance.

cerebrum [sə·rē'·brəm]: *n.* The largest part of the brain; it receives and interprets signals from sense organs, sends signals to muscles, and is the center for thinking, memory, imagination, and decisions.

cone cells [kōn selz]: *n.* Cone-shaped nerve cells in the retina that allow color vision.

eardrum [ēr'·drum]: *n.* The thin layer of tissue that separates the outer ear and the middle ear; sound causes it to vibrate and these vibrations pass to the small bones of the middle ear.

lens [lenz]: *n.* The part of the eye that focuses light rays on the retina.

nerve cell [nûrv sel]: *n.* The basic unit of living matter that makes up all parts of the nervous system.

nerves [nûrvz]: *n.* Cordlike bundles of nerve cells that connect all parts of the body with the brain and spinal cord.

nervous system [nûr'·vəs sis'·təm]: *n.* The body's control system, made up of the sense organs, brain, spinal cord, and nerves.

pupil [pyōō'·pəl]: *n.* The opening that allows light to enter the eye; it is the dark spot in the center of the eye.

reaction time [rē·ak'·shən tīm]: *n.* The time it takes for a person to perform an action in response to signals from a sense organ.

reflex action [rē'·fleks ak'·shən]: *n.* An action that takes place extremely rapidly when signals between a sense organ and muscle connect in the spinal cord.

retina [ret'·ən·ə]: *n.* A layer of nerve cells that lines the back of the eyeball; when light falls on the retina, the nerve cells send signals that travel over the seeing nerve to the vision center of the brain.

rod cells [rod selz]: *n.* Rod-shaped nerve cells in the retina that allow black-and-white vision.

sense organ [sens ôr'·gən]: *n.* An organ with nerve cells that react to specific things in the environment by sending signals to the brain or spinal cord; the eyes, ears, nose, and parts of the tongue and skin are sense organs.

spinal cord [spīn'·əl kôrd]: *n.* The long, thick cord of nerves that runs down the back of the body and links the brain with most nerves in the body.

taste buds [tāst' budz]: *n.* Structures in the tongue that make it possible to taste.

a	add, map	ī	ice, write	û(r)	burn, term
ā	ace, rate	o	odd, hot	yōō	fuse, few
â(r)	care, air	ō	open, so	ə	a in above
ä	palm, father	ô	order, jaw		e in sicken
e	end, pet	ŏŏ	took, full		i in possible
ē	equal, tree	ōō	pool, food		o in melon
i	it, give	u	up, done		u in circus

INDEX

Page references in *italics* indicate illustrations, photographs, and tables.